RV Camping Journal

Log Your Memories As You Log The Miles

Annell Nelson | Lourdes Welhaven

ISBN-13: 978-1-7944-3030-3

Cover and book design by Welhaven and Associates.
For more information go to www.welhavenandassociates.com

Arrival		Departure	

/ /	:	AM PM	/ /	:	AM PM
Date	Time		Date	Time	

Site #_____ Number of Days Reserved _____

Reservation # _____

Weather _____

Things to do at the camp

Things to do nearby

Restaurants

Wildlife seen

People met

Sites to consider for future visits _____

_____

Ratings

Google_____   Yelp_____   Trip Advisor_____

Campendium_____   Camground Reviews_____   Other_____

My Rating

☆ ☆ ☆ ☆ ☆

Poor ◄————————————► Excellent

_____

Campground Name
_____

Address
_____

City   State/Province   Country   Zip Code
_____

Telephone   Website

❏ Reservations Allowed   ❏ First Come/First Serve

Type of Campground (circle one)

National Forest   State Park   Private   Army Corp of Engineers

County   Bureau of Land Management   Other _____

Rates

Nightly Rate _____   Price Reduced with Longer Stays_____

Extra Daily Entrance Fee _____   Discounts Available_____

Save $ By Purchasing Park Pass _____

Rate Notes _____

Hook Ups	**Restroom**	**Security**

Hook Ups

Electric ❏ Amp_____
Water at Park ❏
Water at Site ❏
Sewer ❏
Dump Station ❏

Laundry

Washer ❏
Dryer ❏

Restroom

Shower ❏   Flush Toilet ❏
Pay Shower ❏   Vault Toilet ❏
Heated ❏   Dry Area ❏
Tokens ❏

Cleanliness: _____

Pets

Pets Allowed ❏ Pet Fee_____

Security

Attendant ❏
Attendant Hours
___ a.m. to ___ pm

Gates ❏
Gates Locked
___ pm to ___ am
Gate Code _____

Connectivity: Cellular Service ❏ Wi-Fi ❏ Cable ❏ Antenna TV Reception ❏

Elevation and terrain _____

Quiet Hours _____

Generator Hours _____

Best time to visit

Winter   Spring   Summer   Fall

Camp Description

_____
_____

	Arrival				Departure	

Arrival / Departure

/ /	:	AM PM		/ /	:	AM PM
Date	Time			Date	Time	

Site #_____ Number of Days Reserved _____

Reservation # _____

Weather _____

Things to do at the camp

Things to do nearby

Restaurants

Wildlife seen

People met

Sites to consider for future visits _____

_____

Ratings

Google_____ Yelp_____ Trip Advisor_____

Campendium_____ Camground Reviews_____ Other_____

My Rating

☆ ☆ ☆ ☆ ☆

Poor ◄————————► Excellent

Campground Name

Address

City   State/Province   Country   Zip Code

Telephone   Website

❑ Reservations Allowed   ❑ First Come/First Serve

Type of Campground (circle one)

National Forest   State Park   Private   Army Corp of Engineers

County   Bureau of Land Management   Other _____

Rates

Nightly Rate _____   Price Reduced with Longer Stays_____

Extra Daily Entrance Fee _____   Discounts Available_____

Save $ By Purchasing Park Pass _____

Rate Notes _____

Hook Ups

Electric ❑ Amp____
Water at Park ❑
Water at Site❑
Sewer ❑
Dump Station ❑

Laundry

Washer ❑
Dryer ❑

Restroom

Shower ❑   Flush Toilet❑
Pay Shower ❑   Vault Toilet ❑
Heated ❑   Dry Area ❑
Tokens ❑

Cleanliness: _____

Pets

Pets Allowed ❑   Pet Fee_____

Security

Attendant ❑
Attendant Hours
___ a.m. to ___ pm

Gates ❑
Gates Locked
___ pm to ___ am
Gate Code _____

Connectivity: Cellular Service❑ Wi-Fi❑ Cable❑ Antenna TV Reception❑

Elevation and terrain _____

Quiet Hours _____

Generator Hours _____

Best time to visit

Winter   Spring   Summer   Fall

Camp Description

	Arrival		Departure
/ /	: AM PM	/ /	: AM PM
Date	Time	Date	Time

Site #_____ Number of Days Reserved _____

Reservation # _____

Weather _____

Things to do at the camp

Things to do nearby

Restaurants

Wildlife seen

People met

Sites to consider for future visits _____

_____

Ratings

Google_____   Yelp_____   Trip Advisor_____

Campendium_____   Camground Reviews_____   Other_____

My Rating

☆ ☆ ☆ ☆ ☆

Poor ⟵——————————⟶ Excellent

Campground Name

Address

City   State/Province   Country   Zip Code

Telephone   Website

❏ Reservations Allowed   ❏ First Come/First Serve

Type of Campground (circle one)
National Forest   State Park   Private   Army Corp of Engineers
County   Bureau of Land Management   Other _____
Rates
Nightly Rate _____   Price Reduced with Longer Stays_____
Extra Daily Entrance Fee _____   Discounts Available_____
Save $ By Purchasing Park Pass _____
Rate Notes _____

Hook Ups

Electric ❏ Amp____
Water at Park ❏
Water at Site ❏
Sewer ❏
Dump Station ❏

Laundry

Washer ❏
Dryer ❏

Restroom

Shower ❏   Flush Toilet ❏
Pay Shower ❏   Vault Toilet ❏
Heated ❏   Dry Area ❏
Tokens ❏

Cleanliness: _____

Pets

Pets Allowed ❏ Pet Fee_____

Security

Attendant ❏
Attendant Hours
___ a.m. to ___ pm

Gates ❏
Gates Locked
___ pm to ___ am
Gate Code _____

Connectivity: Cellular Service ❏ Wi-Fi ❏ Cable ❏ Antenna TV Reception ❏

Elevation and terrain _____

Quiet Hours _____

Generator Hours _____

Best time to visit

Winter   Spring   Summer   Fall

Camp Description

	Arrival				Departure		
/	/	:	AM PM	/	/	:	AM PM
Date	Time			Date	Time		

Site #_____ Number of Days Reserved _____

Reservation # _____

Weather _____

Things to do at the camp

Things to do nearby

Restaurants

Wildlife seen

People met

Sites to consider for future visits _____

_____

Ratings

Google_____   Yelp_____   Trip Advisor_____

Campendium_____   Camground Reviews_____   Other_____

My Rating

☆ ☆ ☆ ☆ ☆

Poor ◄————————————► Excellent

Campground Name

Address

| City | State/Province | Country | Zip Code |

Telephone   Website

❏ Reservations Allowed   ❏ First Come/First Serve

Type of Campground (circle one)

National Forest   State Park   Private   Army Corp of Engineers

County   Bureau of Land Management   Other _____

Rates

Nightly Rate _____   Price Reduced with Longer Stays _____

Extra Daily Entrance Fee _____   Discounts Available_____

Save $ By Purchasing Park Pass _____

Rate Notes _____

Hook Ups

Electric ❏ Amp_____
Water at Park ❏
Water at Site ❏
Sewer ❏
Dump Station ❏

Laundry

Washer ❏
Dryer ❏

Restroom

Shower ❏   Flush Toilet ❏
Pay Shower ❏   Vault Toilet ❏
Heated ❏   Dry Area ❏
Tokens ❏

Cleanliness: _____

Pets

Pets Allowed ❏   Pet Fee_____

Security

Attendant ❏

Attendant Hours
___ a.m. to ___ pm

Gates ❏
Gates Locked
___ pm to ___ am

Gate Code _____

Connectivity: Cellular Service ❏ Wi-Fi ❏ Cable ❏ Antenna TV Reception ❏

Elevation and terrain _____

Quiet Hours _____

Generator Hours _____

Best time to visit

Winter   Spring   Summer   Fall

Camp Description

| |
| |

	Arrival			Departure	
/ /	:	AM PM	/ /	:	AM PM
Date	Time		Date	Time	

Site # _____ Number of Days Reserved _____

Reservation # _____

Weather _____

Things to do at the camp

Things to do nearby

Restaurants

Wildlife seen

People met

Sites to consider for future visits _____

Ratings

Google_____ Yelp_____ Trip Advisor_____

Campendium_____ Camground Reviews_____ Other_____

My Rating

☆ ☆ ☆ ☆ ☆

Poor ⟵─────────⟶ Excellent

_____

Campground Name

_____

Address

_____

City   State/Province   Country   Zip Code

_____

Telephone   Website

❑ Reservations Allowed   ❑ First Come/First Serve

Type of Campground (circle one)
National Forest   State Park   Private   Army Corp of Engineers
County   Bureau of Land Management   Other _____

Rates
Nightly Rate _____   Price Reduced with Longer Stays_____
Extra Daily Entrance Fee _____   Discounts Available_____
Save $ By Purchasing Park Pass _____
Rate Notes _____

Hook Ups

Electric ❑ Amp_____
Water at Park ❑
Water at Site ❑
Sewer ❑
Dump Station ❑

Laundry

Washer ❑
Dryer ❑

Restroom

Shower ❑	Flush Toilet ❑
Pay Shower ❑	Vault Toilet ❑
Heated ❑	Dry Area ❑
Tokens ❑	

Cleanliness: _____

Pets

Pets Allowed ❑   Pet Fee_____

Security

Attendant ❑

Attendant Hours
___ a.m. to ___ pm

Gates ❑
Gates Locked
___ pm to ___ am
Gate Code _____

Connectivity: Cellular Service ❑ Wi-Fi ❑ Cable ❑ Antenna TV Reception ❑

Elevation and terrain _____

Quiet Hours _____

Generator Hours _____

Best time to visit

Winter   Spring   Summer   Fall

Camp Description

Arrival		Departure	
/ /	: AM PM	/ /	: AM PM
Date	Time	Date	Time

Site # _____ Number of Days Reserved _____

Reservation # _____

Weather _____

Things to do at the camp

Things to do nearby

Restaurants

Wildlife seen

People met

Sites to consider for future visits _____

_____

Ratings

Google_____   Yelp_____   Trip Advisor_____

Campendium_____   Camground Reviews_____   Other_____

My Rating

☆ ☆ ☆ ☆ ☆

Poor ←⟶ Excellent

_____

Campground Name

_____

Address

_____

City   State/Province   Country   Zip Code

_____

Telephone   Website

❑ Reservations Allowed   ❑ First Come/First Serve

Type of Campground (circle one)
National Forest   State Park   Private   Army Corp of Engineers
County   Bureau of Land Management   Other _____

Rates
Nightly Rate _____   Price Reduced with Longer Stays_____
Extra Daily Entrance Fee _____   Discounts Available_____
Save $ By Purchasing Park Pass _____
Rate Notes _____

Hook Ups

Electric ❑ Amp_____
Water at Park ❑
Water at Site ❑
Sewer ❑
Dump Station ❑

Laundry

Washer ❑
Dryer ❑

Restroom

Shower ❑   Flush Toilet ❑
Pay Shower ❑   Vault Toilet ❑
Heated ❑   Dry Area ❑
Tokens ❑

Cleanliness: _____

Pets

Pets Allowed ❑   Pet Fee_____

Security

Attendant ❑

Attendant Hours
___ a.m. to ___ pm

Gates ❑
Gates Locked
___ pm to ___ am

Gate Code _____

Connectivity: Cellular Service ❑ Wi-Fi ❑ Cable ❑ Antenna TV Reception ❑

Elevation and terrain _____

Quiet Hours _____

Generator Hours _____

Best time to visit

Winter   Spring   Summer   Fall

Camp Description

	Arrival				Departure		
/	/	:	AM PM	/	/	:	AM PM
Date		Time		Date		Time	

Site #_____ Number of Days Reserved _____

Reservation # _____

Weather _____

Things to do at the camp

Things to do nearby

Restaurants

Wildlife seen

People met

Sites to consider for future visits _____

_____

Ratings

Google_____   Yelp_____   Trip Advisor_____

Campendium_____   Camground Reviews_____   Other_____

My Rating

☆ ☆ ☆ ☆ ☆

Poor ←————————→ Excellent

Campground Name

Address

| City | State/Province | Country | Zip Code |

Telephone   Website

❏ Reservations Allowed   ❏ First Come/First Serve

Type of Campground (circle one)

National Forest   State Park   Private   Army Corp of Engineers

County   Bureau of Land Management   Other _____

Rates

Nightly Rate _____   Price Reduced with Longer Stays_____

Extra Daily Entrance Fee _____   Discounts Available_____

Save $ By Purchasing Park Pass _____

Rate Notes _____

Hook Ups

Electric ❏ Amp____
Water at Park ❏
Water at Site ❏
Sewer ❏
Dump Station ❏

Laundry

Washer ❏
Dryer ❏

Restroom

Shower ❏   Flush Toilet ❏
Pay Shower ❏   Vault Toilet ❏
Heated ❏   Dry Area ❏
Tokens ❏

Cleanliness: _____

Pets

Pets Allowed ❏   Pet Fee_____

Security

Attendant ❏

Attendant Hours
____ a.m. to ____ pm

Gates ❏
Gates Locked
____ pm   to ____ am

Gate Code _____

Connectivity: Cellular Service ❏ Wi-Fi ❏ Cable ❏ Antenna TV Reception ❏

Elevation and terrain _____

Quiet Hours _____

Generator Hours _____

Best time to visit

Winter   Spring   Summer   Fall

Camp Description

Arrival

/ /	:	AM PM
Date	Time	

Departure

/ /	:	AM PM
Date	Time	

Site #_____ Number of Days Reserved _____

Reservation # _____

Weather _____

Things to do at the camp

Things to do nearby

Restaurants

Wildlife seen

People met

Sites to consider for future visits _____

_____

Ratings

Google_____   Yelp_____   Trip Advisor_____

Campendium_____   Camground Reviews_____   Other_____

My Rating

☆ ☆ ☆ ☆ ☆

Poor ←——————————————→ Excellent

_____

Campground Name

_____

Address

_____

City   State/Province   Country   Zip Code

_____

Telephone   Website

❏ Reservations Allowed   ❏ First Come/First Serve

Type of Campground (circle one)
National Forest   State Park   Private   Army Corp of Engineers
County   Bureau of Land Management   Other _____

Rates

Nightly Rate _____   Price Reduced with Longer Stays_____

Extra Daily Entrance Fee _____   Discounts Available_____

Save $ By Purchasing Park Pass _____

Rate Notes _____

Hook Ups

Electric ❏ Amp____
Water at Park ❏
Water at Site ❏
Sewer ❏
Dump Station ❏

Laundry

Washer ❏
Dryer ❏

Restroom

Shower ❏   Flush Toilet ❏
Pay Shower ❏   Vault Toilet ❏
Heated ❏   Dry Area ❏
Tokens ❏

Cleanliness: _____

Pets

Pets Allowed ❏ Pet Fee_____

Security

Attendant ❏

Attendant Hours
___ a.m. to ___ pm

Gates ❏
Gates Locked
___ pm to ___ am
Gate Code _____

Connectivity: Cellular Service ❏ Wi-Fi ❏ Cable ❏ Antenna TV Reception ❏

Elevation and terrain _____

Quiet Hours _____

Generator Hours _____

Best time to visit

Winter   Spring   Summer   Fall

Camp Description

	Arrival			Departure	
/ /		: AM PM	/ /		: AM PM
Date	Time		Date	Time	

Site #_____ Number of Days Reserved _____

Reservation # _____

Weather _____

Things to do at the camp

Things to do nearby

Restaurants

Wildlife seen

People met

Sites to consider for future visits _____

_____

Ratings

Google_____   Yelp_____   Trip Advisor_____

Campendium_____   Camground Reviews_____   Other_____

My Rating

☆ ☆ ☆ ☆ ☆

Poor ⟵——————————⟶ Excellent

Campground Name

Address

City   State/Province   Country   Zip Code

Telephone   Website

☐ Reservations Allowed   ☐ First Come/First Serve

Type of Campground (circle one)

National Forest   State Park   Private   Army Corp of Engineers
County   Bureau of Land Management   Other _____

Rates

Nightly Rate _____   Price Reduced with Longer Stays_____

Extra Daily Entrance Fee _____   Discounts Available_____

Save $ By Purchasing Park Pass _____

Rate Notes _____

Hook Ups

Electric ☐ Amp_____
Water at Park ☐
Water at Site☐
Sewer ☐
Dump Station ☐

Laundry

Washer☐
Dryer ☐

Restroom

Shower ☐   Flush Toilet☐
Pay Shower ☐   Vault Toilet ☐
Heated ☐   Dry Area ☐
Tokens ☐

Cleanliness: _____

Pets

Pets Allowed ☐ Pet Fee_____

Security

Attendant ☐

Attendant Hours
___ a.m. to ___ pm

Gates ☐
Gates Locked
___ pm to ___ am

Gate Code _____

Connectivity: Cellular Service☐ Wi-Fi☐ Cable☐ Antenna TV Reception☐

Elevation and terrain _____

Quiet Hours _____

Generator Hours _____

Best time to visit

Winter   Spring   Summer   Fall

Camp Description

Arrival   Departure

| / /   : | AM PM | | / /   : | AM PM |
| Date   Time | | Date   Time |

Site #_____ Number of Days Reserved _____

Reservation # _____

Weather _____

Things to do at the camp

| |
| |

Things to do nearby

| |
| |

Restaurants

| |
| |

Wildlife seen

| |
| |

People met

| |
| |

Sites to consider for future visits _____

_____

Ratings

Google_____   Yelp_____   Trip Advisor_____

Campendium_____   Camground Reviews_____   Other_____

My Rating

☆ ☆ ☆ ☆ ☆

Poor ◄——————————► Excellent

Campground Name

Address

| City | State/Province | Country | Zip Code |

Telephone

Website

❑ Reservations Allowed   ❑ First Come/First Serve

Type of Campground (circle one)

National Forest   State Park   Private   Army Corp of Engineers

County   Bureau of Land Management   Other _____

Rates

Nightly Rate _____   Price Reduced with Longer Stays_____

Extra Daily Entrance Fee _____   Discounts Available_____

Save $ By Purchasing Park Pass _____

Rate Notes _____

Hook Ups

Electric ❑ Amp____
Water at Park ❑
Water at Site❑
Sewer ❑
Dump Station ❑

Laundry

Washer❑
Dryer ❑

Restroom

Shower ❑   Flush Toilet❑
Pay Shower ❑   Vault Toilet ❑
Heated ❑   Dry Area ❑
Tokens ❑

Cleanliness: _____

Pets

Pets Allowed ❑ Pet Fee_____

Security

Attendant ❑

Attendant Hours
___ a.m. to ___ pm

Gates ❑
Gates Locked
___ pm to ___ am

Gate Code _____

Connectivity: Cellular Service❑ Wi-Fi❑ Cable ❑ Antenna TV Reception❑

Elevation and terrain _____

Quiet Hours _____

Generator Hours _____

Best time to visit

Winter   Spring   Summer   Fall

Camp Description

Arrival	Departure
/ / : AM/PM	/ / : AM/PM
Date Time	Date Time

Site #_____ Number of Days Reserved _____

Reservation # _____

Weather _____

Things to do at the camp

Things to do nearby

Restaurants

Wildlife seen

People met

Sites to consider for future visits _____

_____

Ratings

Google_____   Yelp_____   Trip Advisor_____

Campendium_____   Camground Reviews_____   Other_____

My Rating

☆ ☆ ☆ ☆ ☆

Poor ◄─────────────► Excellent

_____

Campground Name

_____

Address

_____

City   State/Province   Country   Zip Code

_____

Telephone   Website

❑ Reservations Allowed   ❑ First Come/First Serve

Type of Campground (circle one)
National Forest   State Park   Private   Army Corp of Engineers
County   Bureau of Land Management   Other _____

Rates

Nightly Rate _____   Price Reduced with Longer Stays_____

Extra Daily Entrance Fee _____   Discounts Available_____

Save $ By Purchasing Park Pass _____

Rate Notes _____

Hook Ups

Electric ❑ Amp____
Water at Park ❑
Water at Site❑
Sewer ❑
Dump Station ❑

Laundry

Washer ❑
Dryer ❑

Restroom

Shower ❑   Flush Toilet❑
Pay Shower ❑   Vault Toilet ❑
Heated ❑   Dry Area ❑
Tokens ❑

Cleanliness: _____

Pets

Pets Allowed ❑ Pet Fee_____

Security

Attendant ❑

Attendant Hours
___ a.m. to ___ pm

Gates ❑
Gates Locked
___ pm to ___ am
Gate Code _____

Connectivity: Cellular Service❑ Wi-Fi❑ Cable❑ Antenna TV Reception❑

Elevation and terrain _____

Quiet Hours _____

Generator Hours _____

Best time to visit

Winter   Spring   Summer   Fall

Camp Description

_____
_____

Arrival

			:	AM
	/	/		PM

Date   Time

Departure

			:	AM
	/	/		PM

Date   Time

Site #_____ Number of Days Reserved _____

Reservation # _____

Weather _____

Things to do at the camp

Things to do nearby

Restaurants

Wildlife seen

People met

Sites to consider for future visits _____

_____

Ratings

Google_____ Yelp_____ Trip Advisor_____

Campendium_____ Camground Reviews_____ Other_____

My Rating

☆ ☆ ☆ ☆ ☆

Poor ◄————————————————► Excellent

Campground Name

Address

City   State/Province   Country   Zip Code

Telephone   Website

❑ Reservations Allowed   ❑ First Come/First Serve

Type of Campground (circle one)

National Forest   State Park   Private   Army Corp of Engineers

County   Bureau of Land Management   Other _____

Rates

Nightly Rate _____   Price Reduced with Longer Stays_____

Extra Daily Entrance Fee _____   Discounts Available_____

Save $ By Purchasing Park Pass _____

Rate Notes _____

Hook Ups

Electric ❑ Amp_____
Water at Park ❑
Water at Site❑
Sewer ❑
Dump Station ❑

Laundry

Washer ❑
Dryer ❑

Restroom

Shower ❑	Flush Toilet❑
Pay Shower ❑	Vault Toilet ❑
Heated ❑	Dry Area ❑
Tokens ❑	

Cleanliness: _____

Pets

Pets Allowed ❑   Pet Fee_____

Security

Attendant ❑

Attendant Hours
____ a.m. to ____ pm

Gates ❑
Gates Locked
____ pm to ____ am

Gate Code _____

Connectivity: Cellular Service❑ Wi-Fi❑ Cable❑ Antenna TV Reception❑

Elevation and terrain _____

Quiet Hours _____

Generator Hours _____

Best time to visit

Winter   Spring   Summer   Fall

Camp Description

	Arrival			Departure	

/ /	:	AM PM	/ /	:	AM PM
Date	Time		Date	Time	

Site #_____ Number of Days Reserved _____

Reservation # _____

Weather _____

Things to do at the camp

Things to do nearby

Restaurants

Wildlife seen

People met

Sites to consider for future visits _____

_____

Ratings

Google_____   Yelp_____   Trip Advisor_____

Campendium_____   Camground Reviews_____   Other_____

My Rating

☆ ☆ ☆ ☆ ☆

Poor ←——————————→ Excellent

_____

Campground Name

_____

Address

_____

City   State/Province   Country   Zip Code

_____

Telephone   Website

❏ Reservations Allowed   ❏ First Come/First Serve

Type of Campground (circle one)

National Forest   State Park   Private   Army Corp of Engineers

County   Bureau of Land Management   Other _____

Rates

Nightly Rate _____   Price Reduced with Longer Stays_____

Extra Daily Entrance Fee _____   Discounts Available_____

Save $ By Purchasing Park Pass _____

Rate Notes _____

Hook Ups

Electric ❏ Amp_____
Water at Park ❏
Water at Site ❏
Sewer ❏
Dump Station ❏

Laundry

Washer ❏
Dryer ❏

Restroom

Shower ❏   Flush Toilet ❏
Pay Shower ❏   Vault Toilet ❏
Heated ❏   Dry Area ❏
Tokens ❏

Cleanliness: _____

Pets

Pets Allowed ❏ Pet Fee_____

Security

Attendant ❏

Attendant Hours
___ a.m. to ___ pm

Gates ❏
Gates Locked
___ pm to ___ am

Gate Code _____

Connectivity: Cellular Service ❏ Wi-Fi ❏ Cable ❏ Antenna TV Reception ❏

Elevation and terrain _____

Quiet Hours _____

Best time to visit

Generator Hours _____

Winter   Spring   Summer   Fall

Camp Description

_____
_____

	Arrival				Departure		
	/	/	:	AM PM		/	/	:	AM PM

| Date | Time | Date | Time |

Site #_____ Number of Days Reserved _____

Reservation # _____

Weather _____

Things to do at the camp

Things to do nearby

Restaurants

Wildlife seen

People met

Sites to consider for future visits _____

_____

Ratings

Google_____ Yelp_____ Trip Advisor_____

Campendium_____ Camground Reviews_____ Other_____

My Rating

☆ ☆ ☆ ☆ ☆

Poor ⟵—————————⟶ Excellent

Campground Name

Address

City   State/Province   Country   Zip Code

Telephone   Website

❑ Reservations Allowed   ❑ First Come/First Serve

Type of Campground (circle one)
National Forest   State Park   Private   Army Corp of Engineers
County   Bureau of Land Management   Other _____

Rates

Nightly Rate _____   Price Reduced with Longer Stays_____

Extra Daily Entrance Fee _____   Discounts Available_____

Save $ By Purchasing Park Pass _____

Rate Notes _____

Hook Ups	**Restroom**	**Security**

Hook Ups

Electric ❑ Amp_____
Water at Park ❑
Water at Site ❑
Sewer ❑
Dump Station ❑

Laundry

Washer ❑
Dryer ❑

Restroom

Shower ❑   Flush Toilet ❑
Pay Shower ❑   Vault Toilet ❑
Heated ❑   Dry Area ❑
Tokens ❑

Cleanliness: _____

Pets

Pets Allowed ❑   Pet Fee_____

Security

Attendant ❑

Attendant Hours
___ a.m. to ___ pm

Gates ❑
Gates Locked
___ pm to ___ am

Gate Code _____

Connectivity: Cellular Service ❑ Wi-Fi ❑ Cable ❑ Antenna TV Reception ❑

Elevation and terrain _____

Quiet Hours _____

Best time to visit

Generator Hours _____

Winter   Spring   Summer   Fall

Camp Description

	Arrival				Departure		
/ /		:	AM PM	/ /		:	AM PM
Date		Time		Date		Time	

Site #_____ Number of Days Reserved _____

Reservation # _____

Weather _____

Things to do at the camp

Things to do nearby

Restaurants

Wildlife seen

People met

Sites to consider for future visits _____

_____

Ratings

Google_____   Yelp_____   Trip Advisor_____

Campendium_____   Camground Reviews_____   Other_____

My Rating

☆ ☆ ☆ ☆ ☆

Poor ⟵――――――――――⟶ Excellent

_____

Campground Name

_____

Address

_____

City   State/Province   Country   Zip Code

_____

Telephone   Website

❑ Reservations Allowed   ❑ First Come/First Serve

Type of Campground (circle one)
National Forest   State Park   Private   Army Corp of Engineers
County   Bureau of Land Management   Other _____

Rates
Nightly Rate _____   Price Reduced with Longer Stays_____
Extra Daily Entrance Fee _____   Discounts Available_____
Save $ By Purchasing Park Pass _____
Rate Notes _____

Hook Ups
Electric ❑ Amp____
Water at Park ❑
Water at Site❑
Sewer ❑
Dump Station ❑

Laundry
Washer ❑
Dryer ❑

Restroom
Shower ❑   Flush Toilet❑
Pay Shower ❑   Vault Toilet ❑
Heated ❑   Dry Area ❑
Tokens ❑

Cleanliness: _____

Pets
Pets Allowed ❑ Pet Fee_____

Security
Attendant ❑

Attendant Hours
___ a.m. to ___ pm

Gates ❑
Gates Locked
___ pm to ___ am

Gate Code _____

Connectivity: Cellular Service❑ Wi-Fi❑ Cable❑ Antenna TV Reception❑

Elevation and terrain _____

Quiet Hours _____

Generator Hours _____

Best time to visit

Winter   Spring   Summer   Fall

Camp Description

	Arrival				Departure		
/ /		:	AM PM	/ /		:	AM PM
Date		Time		Date		Time	

Site #_____ Number of Days Reserved _____

Reservation # _____

Weather _____

Things to do at the camp

Things to do nearby

Restaurants

Wildlife seen

People met

Sites to consider for future visits _____

_____

Ratings

Google_____   Yelp_____   Trip Advisor_____

Campendium_____   Camground Reviews_____   Other_____

My Rating

☆ ☆ ☆ ☆ ☆

Poor ⟵——————————⟶ Excellent

Campground Name

Address

City   State/Province   Country   Zip Code

Telephone   Website

❏ Reservations Allowed   ❏ First Come/First Serve

Type of Campground (circle one)

National Forest   State Park   Private   Army Corp of Engineers

County   Bureau of Land Management   Other _____

Rates

Nightly Rate _____   Price Reduced with Longer Stays _____

Extra Daily Entrance Fee _____   Discounts Available _____

Save $ By Purchasing Park Pass _____

Rate Notes _____

Hook Ups

Electric ❏ Amp____
Water at Park ❏
Water at Site ❏
Sewer ❏
Dump Station ❏

Laundry

Washer ❏
Dryer ❏

Restroom

Shower ❏   Flush Toilet ❏
Pay Shower ❏   Vault Toilet ❏
Heated ❏   Dry Area ❏
Tokens ❏

Cleanliness: _____

Pets

Pets Allowed ❏   Pet Fee_____

Security

Attendant ❏

Attendant Hours
___ a.m. to ___ pm

Gates ❏
Gates Locked
___ pm to ___ am

Gate Code _____

Connectivity: Cellular Service ❏ Wi-Fi ❏ Cable ❏ Antenna TV Reception ❏

Elevation and terrain _____

Quiet Hours _____

Generator Hours _____

Best time to visit

Winter   Spring   Summer   Fall

Camp Description

Arrival		Departure	

	/	/		:	AM PM		/	/		:	AM PM

Date — Time — Date — Time

Site #_____ Number of Days Reserved _____

Reservation # _____

Weather _____

Things to do at the camp

Things to do nearby

Restaurants

Wildlife seen

People met

Sites to consider for future visits _____

_____

Ratings

Google_____ Yelp_____ Trip Advisor_____

Campendium_____ Camground Reviews_____ Other_____

My Rating

☆ ☆ ☆ ☆ ☆

Poor ←——————————→ Excellent

Campground Name

Address

City | State/Province | Country | Zip Code

Telephone | Website

❑ Reservations Allowed   ❑ First Come/First Serve

Type of Campground (circle one)

National Forest   State Park   Private   Army Corp of Engineers
County   Bureau of Land Management   Other _____

Rates

Nightly Rate _____   Price Reduced with Longer Stays _____

Extra Daily Entrance Fee _____   Discounts Available _____

Save $ By Purchasing Park Pass _____

Rate Notes _____

Hook Ups

Electric ❑ Amp____
Water at Park ❑
Water at Site ❑
Sewer ❑
Dump Station ❑

Laundry

Washer ❑
Dryer ❑

Restroom

Shower ❑   Flush Toilet ❑
Pay Shower ❑   Vault Toilet ❑
Heated ❑   Dry Area ❑
Tokens ❑

Cleanliness: _____

Pets

Pets Allowed ❑ Pet Fee _____

Security

Attendant ❑

Attendant Hours
___ a.m. to ___ pm

Gates ❑
Gates Locked
___ pm to ___ am

Gate Code _____

Connectivity: Cellular Service ❑ Wi-Fi ❑ Cable ❑ Antenna TV Reception ❑

Elevation and terrain _____

Quiet Hours _____

Generator Hours _____

Best time to visit

Winter   Spring   Summer   Fall

Camp Description

	Arrival				Departure		
	/ /	:	AM PM		/ /	:	AM PM
	Date	Time			Date	Time	

Site #_____ Number of Days Reserved _____

Reservation # _____

Weather _____

Things to do at the camp

Things to do nearby

Restaurants

Wildlife seen

People met

Sites to consider for future visits _____

_____

Ratings

Google_____ Yelp_____ Trip Advisor_____

Campendium_____ Camground Reviews_____ Other_____

My Rating

☆ ☆ ☆ ☆ ☆

Poor ◄————————► Excellent

_____

Campground Name

_____

Address

_____

City   State/Province   Country   Zip Code

_____

Telephone   Website

❏ Reservations Allowed   ❏ First Come/First Serve

Type of Campground (circle one)

National Forest   State Park   Private   Army Corp of Engineers

County   Bureau of Land Management   Other _____

Rates

Nightly Rate _____   Price Reduced with Longer Stays_____

Extra Daily Entrance Fee _____   Discounts Available_____

Save $ By Purchasing Park Pass _____

Rate Notes _____

Hook Ups

Electric ❏ Amp_____
Water at Park ❏
Water at Site ❏
Sewer ❏
Dump Station ❏

Laundry

Washer ❏
Dryer ❏

Restroom

Shower ❏   Flush Toilet ❏
Pay Shower ❏   Vault Toilet ❏
Heated ❏   Dry Area ❏
Tokens ❏

Cleanliness: _____

Pets

Pets Allowed ❏ Pet Fee_____

Security

Attendant ❏

Attendant Hours
____ a.m. to ____ pm

Gates ❏
Gates Locked
____ pm to ____ am

Gate Code _____

Connectivity: Cellular Service ❏ Wi-Fi ❏ Cable ❏ Antenna TV Reception ❏

Elevation and terrain _____

Quiet Hours _____

Generator Hours _____

Best time to visit

Winter   Spring   Summer   Fall

Camp Description

	Arrival			Departure	
/ /	:	AM PM	/ /	:	AM PM
Date	Time		Date	Time	

Site #_____ Number of Days Reserved _____

Reservation # _____

Weather _____

Things to do at the camp

Things to do nearby

Restaurants

Wildlife seen

People met

Sites to consider for future visits _____

_____

Ratings

Google_____ Yelp_____ Trip Advisor_____

Campendium_____ Camground Reviews_____ Other_____

My Rating

☆ ☆ ☆ ☆ ☆

Poor ← ——————————— → Excellent

_____

Campground Name

_____

Address

_____

City   State/Province   Country   Zip Code

_____

Telephone   Website

❏ Reservations Allowed   ❏ First Come/First Serve

Type of Campground (circle one)
National Forest   State Park   Private   Army Corp of Engineers
County   Bureau of Land Management   Other _____

Rates
Nightly Rate _____   Price Reduced with Longer Stays _____
Extra Daily Entrance Fee _____   Discounts Available_____
Save $ By Purchasing Park Pass _____
Rate Notes _____

Hook Ups
Electric ❏ Amp_____
Water at Park ❏
Water at Site ❏
Sewer ❏
Dump Station ❏

Laundry
Washer ❏
Dryer ❏

Restroom
Shower ❏   Flush Toilet ❏
Pay Shower ❏   Vault Toilet ❏
Heated ❏   Dry Area ❏
Tokens ❏

Cleanliness: _____

Pets
Pets Allowed ❏   Pet Fee_____

Security
Attendant ❏
Attendant Hours
___ a.m. to ___ pm

Gates ❏
Gates Locked
___ pm to ___ am
Gate Code _____

Connectivity: Cellular Service ❏ Wi-Fi ❏ Cable ❏ Antenna TV Reception ❏

Elevation and terrain _____

Quiet Hours _____

Generator Hours _____

Best time to visit

Winter   Spring   Summer   Fall

Camp Description

_____
_____

	Arrival			Departure	
	/ /	:	AM PM		/ /	:	AM PM
	Date	Time		Date	Time

Site #_____ Number of Days Reserved _____

Reservation # _____

Weather _____

Things to do at the camp

Things to do nearby

Restaurants

Wildlife seen

People met

Sites to consider for future visits _____

_____

Ratings

Google_____ Yelp_____ Trip Advisor_____

Campendium_____ Camground Reviews_____ Other_____

My Rating

☆ ☆ ☆ ☆ ☆

Poor ◄———————————► Excellent

Campground Name

Address

| City | State/Province | Country | Zip Code |

Telephone   Website

☐ Reservations Allowed   ☐ First Come/First Serve

Type of Campground (circle one)

National Forest   State Park   Private   Army Corp of Engineers

County   Bureau of Land Management   Other _____

Rates

Nightly Rate _____   Price Reduced with Longer Stays_____

Extra Daily Entrance Fee _____   Discounts Available_____

Save $ By Purchasing Park Pass _____

Rate Notes _____

Hook Ups

Electric ☐ Amp_____
Water at Park ☐
Water at Site ☐
Sewer ☐
Dump Station ☐

Laundry

Washer ☐
Dryer ☐

Restroom

Shower ☐   Flush Toilet ☐
Pay Shower ☐   Vault Toilet ☐
Heated ☐   Dry Area ☐
Tokens ☐

Cleanliness: _____

Pets

Pets Allowed ☐   Pet Fee_____

Security

Attendant ☐
Attendant Hours
___ a.m. to ___ pm

Gates ☐
Gates Locked
___ pm to ___ am

Gate Code _____

Connectivity: Cellular Service ☐ Wi-Fi ☐ Cable ☐ Antenna TV Reception ☐

Elevation and terrain _____

Quiet Hours _____

Generator Hours _____

Best time to visit

Winter   Spring   Summer   Fall

Camp Description

	Arrival				Departure		
/	/	:	AM PM	/	/	:	AM PM
Date		Time		Date		Time	

Site #_____ Number of Days Reserved _____

Reservation # _____

Weather _____

Things to do at the camp

Things to do nearby

Restaurants

Wildlife seen

People met

Sites to consider for future visits _____

_____

Ratings

Google_____   Yelp_____   Trip Advisor_____

Campendium_____   Camground Reviews_____   Other_____

My Rating

☆ ☆ ☆ ☆ ☆

Poor ◄————————————► Excellent

Campground Name

Address

| City | State/Province | Country | Zip Code |

Telephone   Website

❑ Reservations Allowed   ❑ First Come/First Serve

Type of Campground (circle one)
National Forest   State Park   Private   Army Corp of Engineers County   Bureau of Land Management   Other _____
Rates
Nightly Rate _____   Price Reduced with Longer Stays_____
Extra Daily Entrance Fee _____   Discounts Available_____
Save $ By Purchasing Park Pass _____
Rate Notes _____

Hook Ups
Electric ❑ Amp____
Water at Park ❑
Water at Site ❑
Sewer ❑
Dump Station ❑

Laundry
Washer ❑
Dryer ❑

Restroom
Shower ❑   Flush Toilet ❑
Pay Shower ❑   Vault Toilet ❑
Heated ❑   Dry Area ❑
Tokens ❑

Cleanliness: _____

Pets
Pets Allowed ❑   Pet Fee_____

Security
Attendant ❑
Attendant Hours
___ a.m. to ___ pm

Gates ❑
Gates Locked
___ pm to ___ am
Gate Code _____

Connectivity: Cellular Service ❑ Wi-Fi ❑ Cable ❑ Antenna TV Reception ❑

Elevation and terrain _____

Quiet Hours _____

Generator Hours _____

Best time to visit
Winter   Spring   Summer   Fall

Camp Description

Arrival		Departure	
/ /	: AM PM	/ /	: AM PM
Date	Time	Date	Time

Site #_____ Number of Days Reserved _____

Reservation # _____

Weather _____

Things to do at the camp

Things to do nearby

Restaurants

Wildlife seen

People met

Sites to consider for future visits _____

_____

Ratings

Google_____ Yelp_____ Trip Advisor_____

Campendium_____ Camground Reviews_____ Other_____

My Rating

☆ ☆ ☆ ☆ ☆

Poor ◄————————————► Excellent

Campground Name

Address _____

City _____ State/Province _____ Country _____ Zip Code _____

Telephone _____ Website _____

❑ Reservations Allowed   ❑ First Come/First Serve

Type of Campground (circle one)
National Forest   State Park   Private   Army Corp of Engineers County   Bureau of Land Management   Other _____
Rates
Nightly Rate _____   Price Reduced with Longer Stays _____ Extra Daily Entrance Fee _____   Discounts Available_____ Save $ By Purchasing Park Pass _____ Rate Notes _____

Hook Ups
Electric ❑ Amp_____
Water at Park ❑
Water at Site ❑
Sewer ❑
Dump Station ❑

Laundry
Washer ❑
Dryer ❑

Restroom
Shower ❑	Flush Toilet ❑
Pay Shower ❑	Vault Toilet ❑
Heated ❑	Dry Area ❑
Tokens ❑	

Cleanliness: _____

Pets
Pets Allowed ❑   Pet Fee_____

Security
Attendant ❑

Attendant Hours
___ a.m. to ___ pm

Gates ❑
Gates Locked
___ pm to ___ am
Gate Code _____

Connectivity: Cellular Service ❑ Wi-Fi ❑ Cable ❑ Antenna TV Reception ❑

Elevation and terrain _____

Quiet Hours _____

Generator Hours _____

Best time to visit
Winter   Spring   Summer   Fall

Camp Description

	Arrival			Departure	
/ /	:	AM PM	/ /	:	AM PM
Date	Time		Date	Time	

Site #_____ Number of Days Reserved _____

Reservation # _____

Weather _____

Things to do at the camp

Things to do nearby

Restaurants

Wildlife seen

People met

Sites to consider for future visits _____

_____

Ratings

Google_____ Yelp_____ Trip Advisor_____

Campendium_____ Camground Reviews_____ Other_____

My Rating

☆ ☆ ☆ ☆ ☆

Poor ◄————————————► Excellent

_____

Campground Name

_____

Address

_____

City   State/Province   Country   Zip Code

_____

Telephone   Website

❏ Reservations Allowed   ❏ First Come/First Serve

Type of Campground (circle one)
National Forest   State Park   Private   Army Corp of Engineers
County   Bureau of Land Management   Other _____
Rates
Nightly Rate _____   Price Reduced with Longer Stays_____
Extra Daily Entrance Fee _____   Discounts Available_____
Save $ By Purchasing Park Pass _____
Rate Notes _____

Hook Ups

Electric ❏ Amp_____
Water at Park ❏
Water at Site❏
Sewer ❏
Dump Station ❏

Laundry

Washer❏
Dryer ❏

Restroom

Shower ❏   Flush Toilet❏
Pay Shower ❏   Vault Toilet ❏
Heated ❏   Dry Area ❏
Tokens ❏

Cleanliness: _____

Pets

Pets Allowed ❏   Pet Fee_____

Security

Attendant ❏

Attendant Hours
___ a.m. to ___ pm

Gates ❏
Gates Locked
___ pm to ___ am
Gate Code _____

Connectivity: Cellular Service❏ Wi-Fi❏ Cable ❏ Antenna TV Reception❏

Elevation and terrain _____

Quiet Hours _____

Generator Hours _____

Best time to visit

Winter   Spring   Summer   Fall

Camp Description

	Arrival		Departure	

Arrival
/ /	:	AM PM
Date	Time	

Departure
/ /	:	AM PM
Date	Time	

Site #_____ Number of Days Reserved _____

Reservation # _____

Weather _____

Things to do at the camp

Things to do nearby

Restaurants

Wildlife seen

People met

Sites to consider for future visits _____

_____

Ratings

Google_____ Yelp_____ Trip Advisor_____

Campendium_____ Camground Reviews_____ Other_____

My Rating

☆ ☆ ☆ ☆ ☆

Poor ⟵———————⟶ Excellent

_____

Campground Name

_____
Address

_____
City   State/Province   Country   Zip Code

_____
Telephone   Website

❑ Reservations Allowed   ❑ First Come/First Serve

Type of Campground (circle one)

National Forest   State Park   Private   Army Corp of Engineers
County   Bureau of Land Management   Other _____

Rates

Nightly Rate _____   Price Reduced with Longer Stays_____

Extra Daily Entrance Fee _____   Discounts Available_____

Save $ By Purchasing Park Pass _____

Rate Notes _____

Hook Ups

Electric ❑ Amp_____
Water at Park ❑
Water at Site❑
Sewer ❑
Dump Station ❑

Laundry
Washer❑
Dryer ❑

Restroom

Shower ❑   Flush Toilet❑
Pay Shower ❑   Vault Toilet ❑
Heated ❑   Dry Area ❑
Tokens ❑

Cleanliness: _____

Pets
Pets Allowed ❑ Pet Fee_____

Security

Attendant ❑
Attendant Hours
___ a.m. to ___ pm

Gates ❑
Gates Locked
___ pm to ___ am
Gate Code _____

Connectivity: Cellular Service❑ Wi-Fi❑ Cable ❑ Antenna TV Reception❑

Elevation and terrain _____

Quiet Hours _____

Generator Hours _____

Best time to visit
Winter   Spring   Summer   Fall

Camp Description

| | Arrival | | | | Departure | | |
| Date | / / | Time | : | AM / PM | Date | / / | Time | : | AM / PM |

Site #_____ Number of Days Reserved _____

Reservation # _____

Weather _____

Things to do at the camp

| |
| |
| |

Things to do nearby

| |
| |
| |

Restaurants

| |
| |
| |

Wildlife seen

| |
| |
| |

People met

| |
| |
| |

Sites to consider for future visits _____

_____

Ratings

Google_____ Yelp_____ Trip Advisor_____

Campendium_____ Camground Reviews_____ Other_____

My Rating

☆ ☆ ☆ ☆ ☆

Poor ◄─────────────► Excellent

Campground Name

Address

| City | State/Province | Country | Zip Code |

Telephone   Website

☐ Reservations Allowed   ☐ First Come/First Serve

Type of Campground (circle one)
National Forest   State Park   Private   Army Corp of Engineers
County   Bureau of Land Management   Other _____
Rates
Nightly Rate _____   Price Reduced with Longer Stays _____
Extra Daily Entrance Fee _____   Discounts Available_____
Save $ By Purchasing Park Pass _____
Rate Notes _____

Hook Ups	**Restroom**	**Security**
Electric ☐ Amp_____	Shower ☐ Flush Toilet ☐	Attendant ☐
Water at Park ☐	Pay Shower ☐ Vault Toilet ☐	Attendant Hours
Water at Site ☐	Heated ☐ Dry Area ☐	___ a.m. to ___ pm
Sewer ☐	Tokens ☐	
Dump Station ☐	Cleanliness: _____	Gates ☐
Laundry		Gates Locked
Washer ☐	**Pets**	___ pm to ___ am
Dryer ☐	Pets Allowed ☐ Pet Fee_____	Gate Code _____

Connectivity: Cellular Service ☐ Wi-Fi ☐ Cable ☐ Antenna TV Reception ☐

Elevation and terrain _____

Quiet Hours _____

Generator Hours _____

Best time to visit

Winter   Spring   Summer   Fall

Camp Description

Arrival

	/	/		:	AM PM
	Date			Time	

Departure

	/	/		:	AM PM
	Date			Time	

Site #_____ Number of Days Reserved _____

Reservation # _____

Weather _____

Things to do at the camp

Things to do nearby

Restaurants

Wildlife seen

People met

Sites to consider for future visits _____

_____

Ratings

Google_____ Yelp_____ Trip Advisor_____

Campendium_____ Camground Reviews_____ Other_____

My Rating

☆ ☆ ☆ ☆ ☆

Poor ⟵————————⟶ Excellent

Campground Name

Address

| City | State/Province | Country | Zip Code |

Telephone   Website

❏ Reservations Allowed   ❏ First Come/First Serve

Type of Campground (circle one)

National Forest   State Park   Private   Army Corp of Engineers

County   Bureau of Land Management   Other _____

Rates

Nightly Rate _____   Price Reduced with Longer Stays_____

Extra Daily Entrance Fee _____   Discounts Available_____

Save $ By Purchasing Park Pass _____

Rate Notes _____

Hook Ups

Electric ❏ Amp_____
Water at Park ❏
Water at Site ❏
Sewer ❏
Dump Station ❏

Laundry

Washer ❏
Dryer ❏

Restroom

Shower ❏   Flush Toilet ❏
Pay Shower ❏   Vault Toilet ❏
Heated ❏   Dry Area ❏
Tokens ❏

Cleanliness: _____

Pets

Pets Allowed ❏   Pet Fee_____

Security

Attendant ❏

Attendant Hours
___ a.m. to ___ pm

Gates ❏
Gates Locked
___ pm to ___ am

Gate Code _____

Connectivity: Cellular Service ❏ Wi-Fi ❏ Cable ❏ Antenna TV Reception ❏

Elevation and terrain _____

Quiet Hours _____

Generator Hours _____

Best time to visit

Winter   Spring   Summer   Fall

Camp Description

Arrival

/ /	:	AM
Date	Time	PM

Departure

/ /	:	AM
Date	Time	PM

Site #_____ Number of Days Reserved _____

Reservation # _____

Weather _____

Things to do at the camp

Things to do nearby

Restaurants

Wildlife seen

People met

Sites to consider for future visits _____

_____

Ratings

Google_____   Yelp_____   Trip Advisor_____

Campendium_____   Camground Reviews_____   Other_____

My Rating

☆ ☆ ☆ ☆ ☆

Poor ⟵——————————⟶ Excellent

_____

Campground Name

_____

Address

_____

City   State/Province   Country   Zip Code

_____

Telephone   Website

☐ Reservations Allowed   ☐ First Come/First Serve

Type of Campground (circle one)
National Forest   State Park   Private   Army Corp of Engineers
County   Bureau of Land Management   Other _____

Rates

Nightly Rate _____   Price Reduced with Longer Stays_____

Extra Daily Entrance Fee _____   Discounts Available_____

Save $ By Purchasing Park Pass _____

Rate Notes _____

Hook Ups
Electric ☐ Amp_____
Water at Park ☐
Water at Site ☐
Sewer ☐
Dump Station ☐

Laundry
Washer ☐
Dryer ☐

Restroom
Shower ☐   Flush Toilet ☐
Pay Shower ☐   Vault Toilet ☐
Heated ☐   Dry Area ☐
Tokens ☐

Cleanliness: _____

Pets
Pets Allowed ☐ Pet Fee_____

Security
Attendant ☐
Attendant Hours
___ a.m. to ___ pm

Gates ☐
Gates Locked
___ pm to ___ am
Gate Code _____

Connectivity: Cellular Service ☐ Wi-Fi ☐ Cable ☐ Antenna TV Reception ☐

Elevation and terrain _____

Quiet Hours _____

Generator Hours _____

Best time to visit

Winter   Spring   Summer   Fall

Camp Description

Arrival		Departure	

Arrival

/ / : AM PM

Date   Time

Departure

/ / : AM PM

Date   Time

Site #_____ Number of Days Reserved _____

Reservation # _____

Weather _____

Things to do at the camp

Things to do nearby

Restaurants

Wildlife seen

People met

Sites to consider for future visits _____

_____

Ratings

Google_____   Yelp_____   Trip Advisor_____

Campendium_____   Camground Reviews_____   Other_____

My Rating

☆ ☆ ☆ ☆ ☆

Poor ←――――――――→ Excellent

_____

Campground Name

_____

Address

_____

City   State/Province   Country   Zip Code

_____

Telephone   Website

❏ Reservations Allowed   ❏ First Come/First Serve

Type of Campground (circle one)
National Forest   State Park   Private   Army Corp of Engineers
County   Bureau of Land Management   Other _____
Rates
Nightly Rate _____   Price Reduced with Longer Stays_____
Extra Daily Entrance Fee _____   Discounts Available_____
Save $ By Purchasing Park Pass _____
Rate Notes _____

Hook Ups
Electric ❏ Amp____
Water at Park ❏
Water at Site ❏
Sewer ❏
Dump Station ❏
Laundry
Washer ❏
Dryer ❏

Restroom
Shower ❏   Flush Toilet ❏
Pay Shower ❏   Vault Toilet ❏
Heated ❏   Dry Area ❏
Tokens ❏

Cleanliness: _____

Pets
Pets Allowed ❏   Pet Fee_____

Security
Attendant ❏
Attendant Hours
____ a.m. to ___ pm

Gates ❏
Gates Locked
____ pm to ___ am
Gate Code _____

Connectivity: Cellular Service ❏ Wi-Fi ❏ Cable ❏ Antenna TV Reception ❏

Elevation and terrain _____

Quiet Hours _____

Generator Hours _____

Best time to visit
Winter   Spring   Summer   Fall

Camp Description

Arrival		Departure	
/ / : AM PM		/ / : AM PM	
Date	Time	Date	Time

Site #_____ Number of Days Reserved _____

Reservation # _____

Weather _____

Things to do at the camp

Things to do nearby

Restaurants

Wildlife seen

People met

Sites to consider for future visits _____

_____

Ratings

Google_____ Yelp_____ Trip Advisor_____

Campendium_____ Camground Reviews_____ Other_____

My Rating

☆ ☆ ☆ ☆ ☆

Poor ⟵————————⟶ Excellent

_____

Campground Name
_____

Address
_____

City   State/Province   Country   Zip Code
_____

Telephone   Website

❑ Reservations Allowed   ❑ First Come/First Serve

Type of Campground (circle one)

National Forest   State Park   Private   Army Corp of Engineers

County   Bureau of Land Management   Other _____

Rates

Nightly Rate _____   Price Reduced with Longer Stays_____

Extra Daily Entrance Fee _____   Discounts Available_____

Save $ By Purchasing Park Pass _____

Rate Notes _____

Hook Ups	**Restroom**		**Security**

Hook Ups

Electric ❑ Amp____
Water at Park ❑
Water at Site ❑
Sewer ❑
Dump Station ❑

Laundry
Washer ❑
Dryer ❑

Restroom

Shower ❑   Flush Toilet ❑
Pay Shower ❑   Vault Toilet ❑
Heated ❑   Dry Area ❑
Tokens ❑

Cleanliness: _____

Pets
Pets Allowed ❑   Pet Fee_____

Security
Attendant ❑

Attendant Hours
___ a.m. to ___ pm

Gates ❑
Gates Locked
___ pm to ___ am

Gate Code _____

Connectivity: Cellular Service ❑ Wi-Fi ❑ Cable ❑ Antenna TV Reception ❑

Elevation and terrain _____

Quiet Hours _____

Generator Hours _____

Best time to visit

Winter   Spring   Summer   Fall

Camp Description

Arrival		Departure	
/ / : AM / PM		/ / : AM / PM	
Date	Time	Date	Time

Site #_____ Number of Days Reserved _____

Reservation # _____

Weather _____

Things to do at the camp

Things to do nearby

Restaurants

Wildlife seen

People met

Sites to consider for future visits _____

Ratings

Google_____ Yelp_____ Trip Advisor_____

Campendium_____ Camground Reviews_____ Other_____

My Rating

☆ ☆ ☆ ☆ ☆

Poor ◄————————————► Excellent

_____

Campground Name

_____

Address

_____

City   State/Province   Country   Zip Code

_____

Telephone   Website

❑ Reservations Allowed   ❑ First Come/First Serve

Type of Campground (circle one)

National Forest   State Park   Private   Army Corp of Engineers

County   Bureau of Land Management   Other _____

Rates

Nightly Rate _____   Price Reduced with Longer Stays_____

Extra Daily Entrance Fee _____   Discounts Available_____

Save $ By Purchasing Park Pass _____

Rate Notes _____

Hook Ups	**Restroom**	**Security**

Hook Ups

Electric ❑ Amp____
Water at Park ❑
Water at Site ❑
Sewer ❑
Dump Station ❑

Laundry

Washer ❑
Dryer ❑

Restroom

Shower ❑   Flush Toilet ❑
Pay Shower ❑   Vault Toilet ❑
Heated ❑   Dry Area ❑
Tokens ❑

Cleanliness: _____

Pets

Pets Allowed ❑   Pet Fee_____

Security

Attendant ❑

Attendant Hours
___ a.m. to ___ pm

Gates ❑
Gates Locked
___ pm to ___ am

Gate Code _____

Connectivity: Cellular Service ❑ Wi-Fi ❑ Cable ❑ Antenna TV Reception ❑

Elevation and terrain _____

Quiet Hours _____

Generator Hours _____

Best time to visit

Winter   Spring   Summer   Fall

Camp Description

_____
_____

Arrival

/	/	:	AM / PM
Date		Time	

Departure

/	/	:	AM / PM
Date		Time	

Site #_____ Number of Days Reserved _____

Reservation # _____

Weather _____

Things to do at the camp

Things to do nearby

Restaurants

Wildlife seen

People met

Sites to consider for future visits _____

_____

Ratings

Google_____ Yelp_____ Trip Advisor_____

Campendium_____ Camground Reviews_____ Other_____

My Rating

☆ ☆ ☆ ☆ ☆

Poor ←————————————→ Excellent

Campground Name

Address

| City | State/Province | Country | Zip Code |

Telephone   Website

❏ Reservations Allowed   ❏ First Come/First Serve

Type of Campground (circle one)

National Forest   State Park   Private   Army Corp of Engineers

County   Bureau of Land Management   Other _____

Rates

Nightly Rate _____   Price Reduced with Longer Stays_____

Extra Daily Entrance Fee _____   Discounts Available_____

Save $ By Purchasing Park Pass _____

Rate Notes _____

Hook Ups

Electric ❏ Amp_____
Water at Park ❏
Water at Site ❏
Sewer ❏
Dump Station ❏

Laundry

Washer ❏
Dryer ❏

Restroom

Shower ❏   Flush Toilet ❏
Pay Shower ❏   Vault Toilet ❏
Heated ❏   Dry Area ❏
Tokens ❏

Cleanliness: _____

Pets

Pets Allowed ❏   Pet Fee_____

Security

Attendant ❏

Attendant Hours
___ a.m. to ___ pm

Gates ❏
Gates Locked
___ pm to ___ am

Gate Code _____

Connectivity: Cellular Service ❏ Wi-Fi ❏ Cable ❏ Antenna TV Reception ❏

Elevation and terrain _____

Quiet Hours _____

Generator Hours _____

Best time to visit

Winter   Spring   Summer   Fall

Camp Description

Arrival

/	/	:	AM PM
Date		Time	

Departure

/	/	:	AM PM
Date		Time	

Site #_____ Number of Days Reserved _____

Reservation # _____

Weather _____

Things to do at the camp

Things to do nearby

Restaurants

Wildlife seen

People met

Sites to consider for future visits _____

_____

Ratings

Google_____ Yelp_____ Trip Advisor_____

Campendium_____ Camground Reviews_____ Other_____

My Rating

☆ ☆ ☆ ☆ ☆

Poor ⟵————————⟶ Excellent

Campground Name

Address

| City | State/Province | Country | Zip Code |

Telephone   Website

❏ Reservations Allowed   ❏ First Come/First Serve

Type of Campground (circle one)

National Forest   State Park   Private   Army Corp of Engineers

County   Bureau of Land Management   Other _____

Rates

Nightly Rate _____   Price Reduced with Longer Stays_____

Extra Daily Entrance Fee _____   Discounts Available_____

Save $ By Purchasing Park Pass _____

Rate Notes _____

Hook Ups

Electric ❏ Amp_____
Water at Park ❏
Water at Site ❏
Sewer ❏
Dump Station ❏

Laundry

Washer ❏
Dryer ❏

Restroom

Shower ❏   Flush Toilet ❏
Pay Shower ❏   Vault Toilet ❏
Heated ❏   Dry Area ❏
Tokens ❏

Cleanliness: _____

Pets

Pets Allowed ❏   Pet Fee_____

Security

Attendant ❏

Attendant Hours
___ a.m. to ___ pm

Gates ❏
Gates Locked
___ pm to ___ am
Gate Code _____

Connectivity: Cellular Service ❏   Wi-Fi ❏   Cable ❏   Antenna TV Reception ❏

Elevation and terrain _____

Quiet Hours _____

Generator Hours _____

Best time to visit

Winter   Spring   Summer   Fall

Camp Description

Arrival	Departure
/ / : AM / PM	/ / : AM / PM
Date Time	Date Time

Site #_____ Number of Days Reserved _____

Reservation # _____

Weather _____

Things to do at the camp

Things to do nearby

Restaurants

Wildlife seen

People met

Sites to consider for future visits _____

_____

Ratings

Google_____   Yelp_____   Trip Advisor_____

Campendium_____   Camground Reviews_____   Other_____

My Rating

☆ ☆ ☆ ☆ ☆

Poor ⟵——————————⟶ Excellent

Campground Name

Address

City   State/Province   Country   Zip Code

Telephone   Website

❏ Reservations Allowed   ❏ First Come/First Serve

Type of Campground (circle one)
National Forest   State Park   Private   Army Corp of Engineers
County   Bureau of Land Management   Other _____

Rates

Nightly Rate _____   Price Reduced with Longer Stays_____

Extra Daily Entrance Fee _____   Discounts Available_____

Save $ By Purchasing Park Pass _____

Rate Notes _____

Hook Ups

Electric ❏ Amp_____
Water at Park ❏
Water at Site ❏
Sewer ❏
Dump Station ❏

Laundry

Washer ❏
Dryer ❏

Restroom

Shower ❏   Flush Toilet ❏
Pay Shower ❏   Vault Toilet ❏
Heated ❏   Dry Area ❏
Tokens ❏

Cleanliness: _____

Pets

Pets Allowed ❏   Pet Fee_____

Security

Attendant ❏

Attendant Hours
___ a.m. to ___ pm

Gates ❏
Gates Locked
___ pm to ___ am

Gate Code _____

Connectivity: Cellular Service ❏ Wi-Fi ❏ Cable ❏ Antenna TV Reception ❏

Elevation and terrain _____

Quiet Hours _____

Generator Hours _____

Best time to visit

Winter   Spring   Summer   Fall

Camp Description

	Arrival				Departure		
/ /	:	AM PM		/ /	:	AM PM	

Arrival — Date — Time

Departure — Date — Time

Site #_____ Number of Days Reserved _____

Reservation # _____

Weather _____

Things to do at the camp

Things to do nearby

Restaurants

Wildlife seen

People met

Sites to consider for future visits _____

_____

Ratings

Google_____ Yelp_____ Trip Advisor_____

Campendium_____ Camground Reviews_____ Other_____

My Rating

☆ ☆ ☆ ☆ ☆

Poor ←——————————→ Excellent

Campground Name

Address

City   State/Province   Country   Zip Code

Telephone   Website

❑ Reservations Allowed   ❑ First Come/First Serve

Type of Campground (circle one)

National Forest   State Park   Private   Army Corp of Engineers

County   Bureau of Land Management   Other _____

Rates

Nightly Rate _____   Price Reduced with Longer Stays _____

Extra Daily Entrance Fee _____   Discounts Available_____

Save $ By Purchasing Park Pass _____

Rate Notes _____

Hook Ups

Electric ❑ Amp____
Water at Park ❑
Water at Site ❑
Sewer ❑
Dump Station ❑

Laundry

Washer ❑
Dryer ❑

Restroom

Shower ❑   Flush Toilet ❑
Pay Shower ❑   Vault Toilet ❑
Heated ❑   Dry Area ❑
Tokens ❑

Cleanliness: _____

Pets

Pets Allowed ❑   Pet Fee_____

Security

Attendant ❑

Attendant Hours
___ a.m. to ___ pm

Gates ❑
Gates Locked
___ pm to ___ am

Gate Code _____

Connectivity: Cellular Service ❑ Wi-Fi ❑ Cable ❑ Antenna TV Reception ❑

Elevation and terrain _____

Quiet Hours _____

Generator Hours _____

Best time to visit

Winter   Spring   Summer   Fall

Camp Description

Arrival		Departure	
/ /	: AM PM	/ /	: AM PM
Date	Time	Date	Time

Site #_____ Number of Days Reserved _____

Reservation # _____

Weather _____

Things to do at the camp

Things to do nearby

Restaurants

Wildlife seen

People met

Sites to consider for future visits _____

_____

Ratings

Google_____   Yelp_____   Trip Advisor_____

Campendium_____   Camground Reviews_____   Other_____

My Rating

☆ ☆ ☆ ☆ ☆

Poor ←——————————→ Excellent

_____

Campground Name

_____

Address

_____

City   State/Province   Country   Zip Code

_____

Telephone   Website

❑ Reservations Allowed   ❑ First Come/First Serve

Type of Campground (circle one)

National Forest   State Park   Private   Army Corp of Engineers

County   Bureau of Land Management   Other _____

Rates

Nightly Rate _____   Price Reduced with Longer Stays_____

Extra Daily Entrance Fee _____   Discounts Available_____

Save $ By Purchasing Park Pass _____

Rate Notes _____

Hook Ups
Electric ❑ Amp_____
Water at Park ❑
Water at Site ❑
Sewer ❑
Dump Station ❑

Laundry
Washer ❑
Dryer ❑

Restroom
Shower ❑   Flush Toilet ❑
Pay Shower ❑   Vault Toilet ❑
Heated ❑   Dry Area ❑
Tokens ❑

Cleanliness: _____

Pets
Pets Allowed ❑ Pet Fee_____

Security
Attendant ❑

Attendant Hours
___ a.m. to ___ pm

Gates ❑
Gates Locked
___ pm to ___ am
Gate Code _____

Connectivity: Cellular Service ❑ Wi-Fi ❑ Cable ❑ Antenna TV Reception ❑

Elevation and terrain _____

Quiet Hours _____

Generator Hours _____

Best time to visit
Winter   Spring   Summer   Fall

Camp Description

Arrival		Departure	
/ /	: AM PM	/ /	: AM PM
Date	Time	Date	Time

Site #_____ Number of Days Reserved _____

Reservation # _____

Weather _____

Things to do at the camp

Things to do nearby

Restaurants

Wildlife seen

People met

Sites to consider for future visits _____

_____

Ratings

Google_____   Yelp_____   Trip Advisor_____

Campendium_____   Camground Reviews_____   Other_____

My Rating

☆ ☆ ☆ ☆ ☆

Poor ←——————————→ Excellent

Campground Name

Address

City   State/Province   Country   Zip Code

Telephone   Website

❏ Reservations Allowed   ❏ First Come/First Serve

Type of Campground (circle one)

National Forest   State Park   Private   Army Corp of Engineers

County   Bureau of Land Management   Other _____

Rates

Nightly Rate _____   Price Reduced with Longer Stays _____

Extra Daily Entrance Fee _____   Discounts Available_____

Save $ By Purchasing Park Pass _____

Rate Notes _____

Hook Ups

Electric ❏ Amp____
Water at Park ❏
Water at Site ❏
Sewer ❏
Dump Station ❏

Laundry

Washer ❏
Dryer ❏

Restroom

Shower	❏	Flush Toilet ❏
Pay Shower	❏	Vault Toilet ❏
Heated	❏	Dry Area ❏
Tokens	❏	

Cleanliness: _____

Pets

Pets Allowed ❏   Pet Fee_____

Security

Attendant ❏

Attendant Hours
____ a.m. to ____ pm

Gates ❏
Gates Locked
____ pm to ____ am

Gate Code _____

Connectivity: Cellular Service ❏   Wi-Fi ❏   Cable ❏   Antenna TV Reception ❏

Elevation and terrain _____

Quiet Hours _____

Generator Hours _____

Best time to visit

Winter   Spring   Summer   Fall

Camp Description

Arrival		Departure	
/ / : AM/PM		/ / : AM/PM	
Date	Time	Date	Time

Site #_____ Number of Days Reserved _____

Reservation # _____

Weather _____

Things to do at the camp

Things to do nearby

Restaurants

Wildlife seen

People met

Sites to consider for future visits _____

_____

Ratings

Google_____ Yelp_____ Trip Advisor_____

Campendium_____ Camground Reviews_____ Other_____

My Rating

☆ ☆ ☆ ☆ ☆

Poor ⟵————————⟶ Excellent

Campground Name

Address

| City | State/Province | Country | Zip Code |

Telephone   Website

❑ Reservations Allowed   ❑ First Come/First Serve

Type of Campground (circle one)

National Forest   State Park   Private   Army Corp of Engineers

County   Bureau of Land Management   Other _____

Rates

Nightly Rate _____   Price Reduced with Longer Stays _____

Extra Daily Entrance Fee _____   Discounts Available_____

Save $ By Purchasing Park Pass _____

Rate Notes _____

Hook Ups

Electric ❑ Amp_____
Water at Park ❑
Water at Site ❑
Sewer ❑
Dump Station ❑

Laundry

Washer ❑
Dryer ❑

Restroom

Shower	❑	Flush Toilet ❑
Pay Shower	❑	Vault Toilet ❑
Heated	❑	Dry Area ❑
Tokens	❑	

Cleanliness: _____

Pets

Pets Allowed ❑   Pet Fee_____

Security

Attendant ❑

Attendant Hours
___ a.m. to ___ pm

Gates ❑

Gates Locked
___ pm to ___ am

Gate Code _____

Connectivity: Cellular Service ❑ Wi-Fi ❑ Cable ❑ Antenna TV Reception ❑

Elevation and terrain _____

Quiet Hours _____

Generator Hours _____

Best time to visit

Winter   Spring   Summer   Fall

Camp Description

Arrival			Departure		
/ /	:	AM PM	/ /	:	AM PM
Date	Time		Date	Time	

Site #_____ Number of Days Reserved _____

Reservation # _____

Weather _____

Things to do at the camp

Things to do nearby

Restaurants

Wildlife seen

People met

Sites to consider for future visits _____

_____

Ratings

Google_____ Yelp_____ Trip Advisor_____

Campendium_____ Camground Reviews_____ Other_____

My Rating

☆ ☆ ☆ ☆ ☆

Poor ←————————————→ Excellent

Campground Name

Address

| City | State/Province | Country | Zip Code |

Telephone   Website

☐ Reservations Allowed   ☐ First Come/First Serve

Type of Campground (circle one)

National Forest   State Park   Private   Army Corp of Engineers

County   Bureau of Land Management   Other _____

Rates

Nightly Rate _____   Price Reduced with Longer Stays_____

Extra Daily Entrance Fee _____   Discounts Available_____

Save $ By Purchasing Park Pass _____

Rate Notes _____

Hook Ups

Electric ☐ Amp_____
Water at Park ☐
Water at Site ☐
Sewer ☐
Dump Station ☐

Laundry

Washer ☐
Dryer ☐

Restroom

Shower ☐   Flush Toilet ☐
Pay Shower ☐   Vault Toilet ☐
Heated ☐   Dry Area ☐
Tokens ☐

Cleanliness: _____

Pets

Pets Allowed ☐   Pet Fee_____

Security

Attendant ☐

Attendant Hours
___ a.m. to ___ pm

Gates ☐
Gates Locked
___ pm to ___ am

Gate Code _____

Connectivity: Cellular Service ☐ Wi-Fi ☐ Cable ☐ Antenna TV Reception ☐

Elevation and terrain _____

Quiet Hours _____

Generator Hours _____

Best time to visit

Winter   Spring   Summer   Fall

Camp Description

Arrival			Departure		

/ /	:	AM PM	/ /	:	AM PM
Date	Time		Date	Time	

Site #_____ Number of Days Reserved _____

Reservation # _____

Weather _____

Things to do at the camp

Things to do nearby

Restaurants

Wildlife seen

People met

Sites to consider for future visits _____

_____

Ratings

Google_____   Yelp_____   Trip Advisor_____

Campendium_____   Camground Reviews_____   Other_____

My Rating

☆ ☆ ☆ ☆ ☆

Poor ◄————————————————► Excellent

Campground Name

Address

City   State/Province   Country   Zip Code

Telephone   Website

❑ Reservations Allowed   ❑ First Come/First Serve

Type of Campground (circle one)

National Forest   State Park   Private   Army Corp of Engineers
County   Bureau of Land Management   Other _____

Rates

Nightly Rate _____   Price Reduced with Longer Stays _____

Extra Daily Entrance Fee _____   Discounts Available _____

Save $ By Purchasing Park Pass _____

Rate Notes _____

Hook Ups
Electric ❑ Amp_____
Water at Park ❑
Water at Site ❑
Sewer ❑
Dump Station ❑

Laundry
Washer ❑
Dryer ❑

Restroom
Shower ❑   Flush Toilet ❑
Pay Shower ❑   Vault Toilet ❑
Heated ❑   Dry Area ❑
Tokens ❑

Cleanliness: _____

Pets
Pets Allowed ❑ Pet Fee_____

Security
Attendant ❑

Attendant Hours
___ a.m. to ___ pm

Gates ❑
Gates Locked
___ pm to ___ am

Gate Code _____

Connectivity: Cellular Service ❑ Wi-Fi ❑ Cable ❑ Antenna TV Reception ❑

Elevation and terrain _____

Quiet Hours _____

Generator Hours _____

Best time to visit

Winter   Spring   Summer   Fall

Camp Description

Arrival		Departure	

| / / | : | AM / PM | | / / | : | AM / PM |

Date   Time   Date   Time

Site #_____ Number of Days Reserved _____

Reservation # _____

Weather _____

Things to do at the camp

Things to do nearby

Restaurants

Wildlife seen

People met

Sites to consider for future visits _____

_____

Ratings

Google_____ Yelp_____ Trip Advisor_____

Campendium_____ Camground Reviews_____ Other_____

My Rating

☆ ☆ ☆ ☆ ☆

Poor ⟵————————⟶ Excellent

_____

Campground Name

_____

Address

_____

City   State/Province   Country   Zip Code

_____

Telephone   Website

❏ Reservations Allowed   ❏ First Come/First Serve

Type of Campground (circle one)
National Forest   State Park   Private   Army Corp of Engineers
County   Bureau of Land Management   Other _____

Rates

Nightly Rate _____   Price Reduced with Longer Stays _____

Extra Daily Entrance Fee _____   Discounts Available_____

Save $ By Purchasing Park Pass _____

Rate Notes _____

Hook Ups

Electric ❏ Amp_____
Water at Park ❏
Water at Site ❏
Sewer ❏
Dump Station ❏

Laundry

Washer ❏
Dryer ❏

Restroom

Shower ❏   Flush Toilet ❏
Pay Shower ❏   Vault Toilet ❏
Heated ❏   Dry Area ❏
Tokens ❏

Cleanliness: _____

Pets

Pets Allowed ❏   Pet Fee_____

Security

Attendant ❏

Attendant Hours
___ a.m. to ___ pm

Gates ❏
Gates Locked
___ pm to ___ am

Gate Code _____

Connectivity: Cellular Service ❏ Wi-Fi ❏ Cable ❏ Antenna TV Reception ❏

Elevation and terrain _____

Quiet Hours _____

Generator Hours _____

Best time to visit

Winter   Spring   Summer   Fall

Camp Description

Arrival

	/		/		:	AM
						PM

Date   Time

Departure

	/		/		:	AM
						PM

Date   Time

Site #_____ Number of Days Reserved _____

Reservation # _____

Weather _____

Things to do at the camp

Things to do nearby

Restaurants

Wildlife seen

People met

Sites to consider for future visits _____

_____

Ratings

Google_____ Yelp_____ Trip Advisor_____

Campendium_____ Camground Reviews_____ Other_____

My Rating

☆ ☆ ☆ ☆ ☆

Poor ⟵——————————⟶ Excellent

Campground Name

Address

City **State/Province** **Country** **Zip Code**

Telephone **Website**

❏ Reservations Allowed ❏ First Come/First Serve

Type of Campground (circle one)

National Forest State Park Private Army Corp of Engineers

County Bureau of Land Management Other _____

Rates

Nightly Rate _____ Price Reduced with Longer Stays _____

Extra Daily Entrance Fee _____ Discounts Available _____

Save $ By Purchasing Park Pass _____

Rate Notes _____

Hook Ups

Electric ❏ Amp_____
Water at Park ❏
Water at Site ❏
Sewer ❏
Dump Station ❏

Laundry

Washer ❏
Dryer ❏

Restroom

Shower ❏ Flush Toilet ❏
Pay Shower ❏ Vault Toilet ❏
Heated ❏ Dry Area ❏
Tokens ❏

Cleanliness: _____

Pets

Pets Allowed ❏ Pet Fee _____

Security

Attendant ❏

Attendant Hours
____ a.m. to ____ pm

Gates ❏
Gates Locked
____ pm to ____ am

Gate Code _____

Connectivity: Cellular Service ❏ Wi-Fi ❏ Cable ❏ Antenna TV Reception ❏

Elevation and terrain _____

Quiet Hours _____

Generator Hours _____

Best time to visit

Winter Spring Summer Fall

Camp Description

Arrival		Departure	
/ /	: AM PM	/ /	: AM PM
Date	Time	Date	Time

Site #_____ Number of Days Reserved _____

Reservation # _____

Weather _____

Things to do at the camp

Things to do nearby

Restaurants

Wildlife seen

People met

Sites to consider for future visits _____

_____

Ratings

Google_____   Yelp_____   Trip Advisor_____

Campendium_____   Camground Reviews_____   Other_____

My Rating

☆ ☆ ☆ ☆ ☆

Poor ⟵————————————⟶ Excellent

_____

Campground Name

_____

Address

_____

City   State/Province   Country   Zip Code

_____

Telephone   Website

❏ Reservations Allowed   ❏ First Come/First Serve

Type of Campground (circle one)
National Forest   State Park   Private   Army Corp of Engineers
County   Bureau of Land Management   Other _____

Rates

Nightly Rate _____   Price Reduced with Longer Stays _____

Extra Daily Entrance Fee _____   Discounts Available_____

Save $ By Purchasing Park Pass _____

Rate Notes _____

Hook Ups
Electric ❏ Amp____
Water at Park ❏
Water at Site ❏
Sewer ❏
Dump Station ❏

Laundry
Washer ❏
Dryer ❏

Restroom
Shower	❏	Flush Toilet	❏
Pay Shower	❏	Vault Toilet	❏
Heated	❏	Dry Area	❏
Tokens	❏		

Cleanliness: _____

Pets
Pets Allowed ❏   Pet Fee_____

Security
Attendant ❏
Attendant Hours
____ a.m. to ____ pm

Gates ❏
Gates Locked
____ pm to ____ am
Gate Code _____

Connectivity: Cellular Service ❏ Wi-Fi ❏ Cable ❏ Antenna TV Reception ❏

Elevation and terrain _____

Quiet Hours _____

Generator Hours _____

Best time to visit

Winter   Spring   Summer   Fall

Camp Description

	Arrival					Departure		
/	/	:	AM PM		/	/	:	AM PM
Date		Time			Date		Time	

Site #_____ Number of Days Reserved _____

Reservation # _____

Weather _____

Things to do at the camp

Things to do nearby

Restaurants

Wildlife seen

People met

Sites to consider for future visits _____

_____

Ratings

Google_____   Yelp_____   Trip Advisor_____

Campendium_____   Camground Reviews_____   Other_____

My Rating

☆ ☆ ☆ ☆ ☆

Poor ⬅————————➡ Excellent

Campground Name

Address

City   State/Province   Country   Zip Code

Telephone   Website

❑ Reservations Allowed   ❑ First Come/First Serve

Type of Campground (circle one)

National Forest   State Park   Private   Army Corp of Engineers

County   Bureau of Land Management   Other _____

Rates

Nightly Rate _____   Price Reduced with Longer Stays_____

Extra Daily Entrance Fee _____   Discounts Available_____

Save $ By Purchasing Park Pass _____

Rate Notes _____

Hook Ups

Electric ❑ Amp_____
Water at Park ❑
Water at Site ❑
Sewer ❑
Dump Station ❑

Laundry
Washer ❑
Dryer ❑

Restroom

Shower ❑   Flush Toilet ❑
Pay Shower ❑   Vault Toilet ❑
Heated ❑   Dry Area ❑
Tokens ❑

Cleanliness: _____

Pets

Pets Allowed ❑   Pet Fee_____

Security

Attendant ❑

Attendant Hours
___ a.m. to ___ pm

Gates ❑
Gates Locked
___ pm to ___ am

Gate Code _____

Connectivity: Cellular Service ❑ Wi-Fi ❑ Cable ❑ Antenna TV Reception ❑

Elevation and terrain _____

Quiet Hours _____

Generator Hours _____

Best time to visit

Winter   Spring   Summer   Fall

Camp Description

Arrival		Departure	
/ / : AM PM		/ / : AM PM	
Date	Time	Date	Time

Site #_____ Number of Days Reserved _____

Reservation # _____

Weather _____

Things to do at the camp

Things to do nearby

Restaurants

Wildlife seen

People met

Sites to consider for future visits _____

_____

Ratings

Google_____ Yelp_____ Trip Advisor_____

Campendium_____ Camground Reviews_____ Other_____

My Rating

☆ ☆ ☆ ☆ ☆

Poor ⟵——————————⟶ Excellent

Campground Name

Address

City   State/Province   Country   Zip Code

Telephone   Website

❑ Reservations Allowed   ❑ First Come/First Serve

Type of Campground (circle one)

National Forest   State Park   Private   Army Corp of Engineers

County   Bureau of Land Management   Other _____

Rates

Nightly Rate _____   Price Reduced with Longer Stays _____

Extra Daily Entrance Fee _____   Discounts Available_____

Save $ By Purchasing Park Pass _____

Rate Notes _____

Hook Ups

Electric ❑ Amp____
Water at Park ❑
Water at Site ❑
Sewer ❑
Dump Station ❑

Laundry

Washer ❑
Dryer ❑

Restroom

Shower ❑   Flush Toilet ❑
Pay Shower ❑   Vault Toilet ❑
Heated ❑   Dry Area ❑
Tokens ❑

Cleanliness: _____

Pets

Pets Allowed ❑   Pet Fee_____

Security

Attendant ❑

Attendant Hours
___ a.m. to ___ pm

Gates ❑
Gates Locked
___ pm to ___ am

Gate Code _____

Connectivity: Cellular Service ❑ Wi-Fi ❑ Cable ❑ Antenna TV Reception ❑

Elevation and terrain _____

Quiet Hours _____

Generator Hours _____

Best time to visit

Winter   Spring   Summer   Fall

Camp Description

Arrival	Departure
/ / ⠀⠀: ⠀AM PM	/ / ⠀⠀: ⠀AM PM
Date⠀⠀⠀⠀Time	Date⠀⠀⠀⠀Time

Site #_____ Number of Days Reserved _____

Reservation # _____

Weather _____

Things to do at the camp

Things to do nearby

Restaurants

Wildlife seen

People met

Sites to consider for future visits _____

Ratings

Google_____ Yelp_____ Trip Advisor_____

Campendium_____ Camground Reviews_____ Other_____

My Rating

☆ ☆ ☆ ☆ ☆

Poor ⟵⟶ Excellent

_____

Campground Name
_____

Address
_____

City   State/Province   Country   Zip Code
_____

Telephone   Website

☐ Reservations Allowed   ☐ First Come/First Serve

Type of Campground (circle one)
National Forest   State Park   Private   Army Corp of Engineers
County   Bureau of Land Management   Other _____

Rates

Nightly Rate _____   Price Reduced with Longer Stays_____

Extra Daily Entrance Fee _____   Discounts Available_____

Save $ By Purchasing Park Pass _____

Rate Notes _____

Hook Ups

Electric ☐ Amp_____
Water at Park ☐
Water at Site ☐
Sewer ☐
Dump Station ☐

Laundry

Washer ☐
Dryer ☐

Restroom

Shower ☐   Flush Toilet ☐
Pay Shower ☐   Vault Toilet ☐
Heated ☐   Dry Area ☐
Tokens ☐

Cleanliness: _____

Pets

Pets Allowed ☐   Pet Fee_____

Security

Attendant ☐

Attendant Hours
___ a.m. to ___ pm

Gates ☐
Gates Locked
___ pm to ___ am

Gate Code _____

Connectivity: Cellular Service ☐ Wi-Fi ☐ Cable ☐ Antenna TV Reception ☐

Elevation and terrain _____

Quiet Hours _____

Generator Hours _____

Best time to visit

Winter   Spring   Summer   Fall

Camp Description

	Arrival			Departure	
/ /	:	AM PM	/ /	:	AM PM
Date	Time		Date	Time	

Site #_____ Number of Days Reserved _____

Reservation # _____

Weather _____

Things to do at the camp

Things to do nearby

Restaurants

Wildlife seen

People met

Sites to consider for future visits _____

_____

Ratings

Google_____   Yelp_____   Trip Advisor_____

Campendium_____   Camground Reviews_____   Other_____

My Rating

☆ ☆ ☆ ☆ ☆

Poor ⟵————————⟶ Excellent

_____

Campground Name

_____

Address

_____

City   State/Province   Country   Zip Code

_____

Telephone   Website

❏ Reservations Allowed   ❏ First Come/First Serve

Type of Campground (circle one)

National Forest   State Park   Private   Army Corp of Engineers

County   Bureau of Land Management   Other _____

Rates

Nightly Rate _____   Price Reduced with Longer Stays_____

Extra Daily Entrance Fee _____   Discounts Available_____

Save $ By Purchasing Park Pass _____

Rate Notes _____

Hook Ups

Electric ❏ Amp____
Water at Park ❏
Water at Site❏
Sewer ❏
Dump Station ❏

Laundry

Washer❏
Dryer ❏

Restroom

Shower ❏   Flush Toilet❏
Pay Shower ❏   Vault Toilet ❏
Heated ❏   Dry Area ❏
Tokens ❏

Cleanliness: _____

Pets

Pets Allowed ❏ Pet Fee_____

Security

Attendant ❏

Attendant Hours
___ a.m. to ___ pm

Gates ❏
Gates Locked
___ pm to ___ am

Gate Code _____

Connectivity: Cellular Service❏ Wi-Fi❏ Cable ❏ Antenna TV Reception❏

Elevation and terrain _____

Quiet Hours _____

Generator Hours _____

Best time to visit

Winter   Spring   Summer   Fall

Camp Description

_____

	Arrival		Departure	

Arrival

| / / | : | AM PM |

Date — Time

Departure

| / / | : | AM PM |

Date — Time

Site #_____ Number of Days Reserved _____

Reservation # _____

Weather _____

Things to do at the camp

| |
| |

Things to do nearby

| |
| |

Restaurants

| |
| |

Wildlife seen

| |
| |

People met

| |
| |

Sites to consider for future visits _____

_____

Ratings

Google_____   Yelp_____   Trip Advisor_____

Campendium_____   Camground Reviews_____   Other_____

My Rating

☆ ☆ ☆ ☆ ☆

Poor ◄————————————► Excellent

_____

Campground Name

_____

Address

_____

City   State/Province   Country   Zip Code

_____

Telephone   Website

❏ Reservations Allowed   ❏ First Come/First Serve

Type of Campground (circle one)
National Forest   State Park   Private   Army Corp of Engineers
County   Bureau of Land Management   Other _____

Rates

Nightly Rate _____   Price Reduced with Longer Stays_____

Extra Daily Entrance Fee _____   Discounts Available_____

Save $ By Purchasing Park Pass _____

Rate Notes _____

Hook Ups	**Restroom**	**Security**
Electric ❏ Amp____	Shower ❏ Flush Toilet❏	Attendant ❏
Water at Park ❏	Pay Shower ❏ Vault Toilet ❏	Attendant Hours
Water at Site❏	Heated ❏ Dry Area ❏	___ a.m. to ___ pm
Sewer ❏	Tokens ❏	
Dump Station ❏	Cleanliness: _____	Gates ❏
Laundry		Gates Locked
Washer ❏	**Pets**	___ pm to ___ am
Dryer ❏	Pets Allowed ❏ Pet Fee_____	Gate Code _____

Connectivity: Cellular Service❏ Wi-Fi❏ Cable❏ Antenna TV Reception❏

Elevation and terrain _____

Quiet Hours _____

Generator Hours _____

Best time to visit

Winter   Spring   Summer   Fall

Camp Description

Arrival		Departure	
/ / :	AM PM	/ / :	AM PM
Date Time		Date Time	

Site #_____ Number of Days Reserved _____

Reservation # _____

Weather _____

Things to do at the camp

Things to do nearby

Restaurants

Wildlife seen

People met

Sites to consider for future visits _____

_____

Ratings

Google_____ Yelp_____ Trip Advisor_____

Campendium_____ Camground Reviews_____ Other_____

My Rating

☆ ☆ ☆ ☆ ☆

Poor ⟵——————————⟶ Excellent

Campground Name

Address

City   State/Province   Country   Zip Code

Telephone   Website

❏ Reservations Allowed   ❏ First Come/First Serve

Type of Campground (circle one)
National Forest   State Park   Private   Army Corp of Engineers County   Bureau of Land Management   Other _____

Rates

Nightly Rate _____   Price Reduced with Longer Stays_____

Extra Daily Entrance Fee _____   Discounts Available_____

Save $ By Purchasing Park Pass _____

Rate Notes _____

Hook Ups

Electric ❏ Amp_____
Water at Park ❏
Water at Site❏
Sewer ❏
Dump Station ❏

Laundry

Washer❏
Dryer ❏

Restroom

Shower ❏	Flush Toilet❏
Pay Shower ❏	Vault Toilet ❏
Heated ❏	Dry Area ❏
Tokens ❏	

Cleanliness: _____

Pets

Pets Allowed ❏   Pet Fee_____

Security

Attendant ❏

Attendant Hours
___ a.m. to ___ pm

Gates ❏
Gates Locked
___ pm to ___ am

Gate Code _____

Connectivity: Cellular Service❏ Wi-Fi❏ Cable❏ Antenna TV Reception❏

Elevation and terrain _____

Quiet Hours _____

Generator Hours _____

Best time to visit

❄ Winter   🍃 Spring   ☀ Summer   🍁 Fall

Camp Description

	Arrival				Departure		
/ /		:	AM	/ /		:	AM
			PM				PM
Date		Time		Date		Time	

Site #_____ Number of Days Reserved _____

Reservation # _____

Weather _____

Things to do at the camp

Things to do nearby

Restaurants

Wildlife seen

People met

Sites to consider for future visits _____

_____

Ratings

Google_____   Yelp_____   Trip Advisor_____

Campendium_____   Camground Reviews_____   Other_____

My Rating

☆ ☆ ☆ ☆ ☆

Poor ◄————————————► Excellent

_____
Campground Name

_____
Address

_____
City   State/Province   Country   Zip Code

_____
Telephone   Website

❑ Reservations Allowed   ❑ First Come/First Serve

Type of Campground (circle one)
National Forest   State Park   Private   Army Corp of Engineers County   Bureau of Land Management   Other _____
Rates
Nightly Rate _____   Price Reduced with Longer Stays _____
Extra Daily Entrance Fee _____   Discounts Available_____
Save $ By Purchasing Park Pass _____
Rate Notes _____

Hook Ups
Electric ❑ Amp____
Water at Park ❑
Water at Site ❑
Sewer ❑
Dump Station ❑
Laundry
Washer ❑
Dryer ❑

Restroom
Shower ❑   Flush Toilet ❑
Pay Shower ❑   Vault Toilet ❑
Heated ❑   Dry Area ❑
Tokens ❑

Cleanliness: _____

Pets
Pets Allowed ❑ Pet Fee_____

Security
Attendant ❑
Attendant Hours
___ a.m. to ___ pm

Gates ❑
Gates Locked
___ pm to ___ am
Gate Code _____

Connectivity: Cellular Service ❑ Wi-Fi ❑ Cable ❑ Antenna TV Reception ❑

Elevation and terrain _____

Quiet Hours _____

Generator Hours _____

Best time to visit

Winter   Spring   Summer   Fall

Camp Description

	Arrival		
	/ /	:	AM PM
	Date	Time	

	Departure		
	/ /	:	AM PM
	Date	Time	

Site #_____ Number of Days Reserved _____

Reservation # _____

Weather _____

Things to do at the camp

Things to do nearby

Restaurants

Wildlife seen

People met

Sites to consider for future visits _____

_____

Ratings

Google_____   Yelp_____   Trip Advisor_____

Campendium_____   Camground Reviews_____   Other_____

My Rating

☆ ☆ ☆ ☆ ☆

Poor ←————————————→ Excellent

Campground Name

Address

City   State/Province   Country   Zip Code

Telephone   Website

❏ Reservations Allowed   ❏ First Come/First Serve

Type of Campground (circle one)

National Forest   State Park   Private   Army Corp of Engineers
County   Bureau of Land Management   Other _____

Rates

Nightly Rate _____   Price Reduced with Longer Stays_____

Extra Daily Entrance Fee _____   Discounts Available_____

Save $ By Purchasing Park Pass _____

Rate Notes _____

Hook Ups

Electric ❏ Amp_____
Water at Park ❏
Water at Site ❏
Sewer ❏
Dump Station ❏

Laundry

Washer ❏
Dryer ❏

Restroom

Shower ❏   Flush Toilet ❏
Pay Shower ❏   Vault Toilet ❏
Heated ❏   Dry Area ❏
Tokens ❏

Cleanliness: _____

Pets

Pets Allowed ❏   Pet Fee_____

Security

Attendant ❏

Attendant Hours
___ a.m. to ___ pm

Gates ❏
Gates Locked
___ pm to ___ am

Gate Code _____

Connectivity: Cellular Service ❏ Wi-Fi ❏ Cable ❏ Antenna TV Reception ❏

Elevation and terrain _____

Quiet Hours _____

Generator Hours _____

Best time to visit

Winter   Spring   Summer   Fall

Camp Description

Arrival

| | : | AM |
|/ /| | PM |

Date   Time

Departure

| | : | AM |
|/ /| | PM |

Date   Time

Site #_____ Number of Days Reserved _____

Reservation # _____

Weather _____

Things to do at the camp

Things to do nearby

Restaurants

Wildlife seen

People met

Sites to consider for future visits _____

_____

Ratings

Google_____   Yelp_____   Trip Advisor_____

Campendium_____   Camground Reviews_____   Other_____

My Rating

☆ ☆ ☆ ☆ ☆

Poor ◄————————————————► Excellent

Campground Name

Address

City   State/Province   Country   Zip Code

Telephone   Website

❏ Reservations Allowed   ❏ First Come/First Serve

Type of Campground (circle one)
National Forest   State Park   Private   Army Corp of Engineers
County   Bureau of Land Management   Other _____

Rates

Nightly Rate _____   Price Reduced with Longer Stays_____

Extra Daily Entrance Fee _____   Discounts Available_____

Save $ By Purchasing Park Pass _____

Rate Notes _____

Hook Ups

Electric ❏ Amp____
Water at Park ❏
Water at Site ❏
Sewer ❏
Dump Station ❏

Laundry

Washer ❏
Dryer ❏

Restroom

Shower ❏   Flush Toilet ❏
Pay Shower ❏   Vault Toilet ❏
Heated ❏   Dry Area ❏
Tokens ❏

Cleanliness: _____

Pets

Pets Allowed ❏ Pet Fee_____

Security

Attendant ❏

Attendant Hours
___ a.m. to ___ pm

Gates ❏
Gates Locked
___ pm to ___ am

Gate Code _____

Connectivity: Cellular Service ❏ Wi-Fi ❏ Cable ❏ Antenna TV Reception ❏

Elevation and terrain _____

Quiet Hours _____

Generator Hours _____

Best time to visit

Winter   Spring   Summer   Fall

Camp Description

	Arrival			Departure	
/ /	:	AM PM	/ /	:	AM PM
Date	Time		Date	Time	

Site #_____ Number of Days Reserved _____

Reservation # _____

Weather _____

Things to do at the camp

Things to do nearby

Restaurants

Wildlife seen

People met

Sites to consider for future visits _____

_____

Ratings

Google_____   Yelp_____   Trip Advisor_____

Campendium_____   Camground Reviews_____   Other_____

My Rating

☆ ☆ ☆ ☆ ☆

Poor ◄————————————► Excellent